SPORTS ALL-STARS

JAMES HARDEN

Anthony K. Hewson

Lerner Publications Company
A division of Lerner Publishing Group, Inc.
241 First Avenue North
Minneapolis, MN 55401 USA

For reading levels and more information, look up this title at www.lernerbooks.com.

Main body text set in Albany Std.
Typeface provided by Agfa.

Library of Congress Cataloging-in-Publication Data
Names: Hewson, Anthony K., author.
Title: James Harden / by Anthony K. Hewson
Description: Minneapolis : Lerner Publications, [2020] | Series: Sports All-Stars |
    Audience: Ages: 7–11. | Audience: Grades: K to Grade 3. | Includes webography. |
    Includes bibliographical references and index.
Identifiers: LCCN 2018059365 (print) | LCCN 2019000349 (ebook) |
    ISBN 9781541556232 (eb pdf) | ISBN 9781541556133 (library binding : alk.
    paper) | ISBN 9781541574496 (paperback : alk. paper)
Subjects: LCSH: Harden, James, 1989-—Juvenile literature. | Basketball players—
    United States—Biography—Juvenile literature.
Classification: LCC GV884.H2435 (ebook) | LCC GV884.H2435 H49 2019 (print) |
    DDC 796.323092 [B] —dc23

LC record available at https://lccn.loc.gov/2018059365

Manufactured in the United States of America
1-CG-7/15/19

CONTENTS

THE MVP

James Harden is a star player for the Houston Rockets.

Houston Rockets star James Harden is famous for his shooting skills on the basketball court. He is also well known for his **bushy** beard and unique clothing choices off the court. Despite his vibrant appearance, he is actually quiet and shy.

FACTS
AT A GLANCE

- **Date of Birth:** August 26, 1989

- **Position:** shooting guard and point guard

- **League:** National Basketball Association (NBA)

- **Professional Highlights:** chosen by the Oklahoma City Thunder as the third overall pick in the 2009 NBA Draft; traded to the Houston Rockets in 2012; scored the most three-point shots in the NBA during the 2017–2018 season; named NBA Most Valuable Player (MVP) in 2018

- **Personal Highlights:** became a top basketball player in high school and college; participates in **charity** work including with his own foundation, 3TheHardenWay; loves fashion

Harden accepts his NBA MVP Award with his mom at his side.

After having a great season in 2017–2018, Harden went to the annual awards show put on by the NBA. He was in the running for the league's MVP Award. He didn't think he'd win, so he didn't write a speech.

But Harden did win. And when he got up to speak, he barely knew what to say. With his mom by his side, Harden grabbed the microphone. He looked out at the room full of his fellow players. "Wow," Harden began. "All glory to God, man. All glory to God. Wow."

Harden had come a long way in his career. He started in the NBA in 2009 as a backup player for Oklahoma City. He was traded to the Rockets in 2012. This helped him show what he could do. Harden finally reached the top of his sport.

During the 2017–2018 season, Harden led the NBA in scoring with 30.4 points per game. The Rockets set a team record with 65 wins that year. The only other basketball players to ever average 30 points while leading a team to 65 wins were Stephen Curry, Michael Jordan, and Kareem Abdul-Jabbar.

To celebrate his MVP season, Harden hosted a party for almost 2,000 people at his old middle school in Los Angeles, California. He wanted to give back to his home community.

Harden high-fives a fan at a party he hosted in his community to celebrate his 2017–2018 season.

BEFORE
THE BEARD

James's mom kisses his cheek after a game.

James Harden was born on August 26, 1989. He grew up near Los Angeles in the city of Compton. Compton was a dangerous place to live. Gang violence and other crime were common.

James was a leader on his high school basketball team.

James was raised by his mother, Monja Willis. She encouraged James and his older brother to play sports. She wanted them to have something positive to do that would keep them out of trouble.

Once James hit the court, he fell in love with basketball. He once wrote a note to his mom that said: "Could u wake up at 7:00. And could u leave me a couple of dollars. —James Harden. P.S. Keep this paper. Imma be a star."

His mom kept the paper. And James kept his promise to be a star.

He led Artesia High School to state titles his junior and senior years. Artesia lost just three games over both years. As a senior James averaged 18.8 points and 7.9 rebounds per game. He was named a McDonald's All-American for being one of the best high school players in the country. He was a top college **prospect**.

James chose Arizona State for college. With James on their team, the Sun Devils improved from an 8–22 record to 21–13. The team was 25–10 the next year and made the national championship tournament. James was named the Pac-10 Conference Player of the Year in 2009.

In 2015, James became the seventh player in Arizona State history to have his jersey number retired. His number 13 was raised to the ceiling at halftime during a Sun Devils game.

James was a star player on his college team, the Arizona State Sun Devils.

James takes a shot during the NBA All-Star Rookie Challenge in 2011.

After those two seasons, he felt ready to make the jump to the NBA.

The Oklahoma City Thunder chose James third overall in the 2009 NBA Draft. The Thunder already had a pair of young stars, Kevin Durant and Russell Westbrook. With James they formed a trio of young talent that rivaled anyone else in the league.

James had a **breakout** third season. He was named the Sixth Man of the Year. This is an award given to the best player who comes off the bench more than he starts. James averaged more than 18 points per game as the Thunder **upset** the San Antonio Spurs in the Western Conference Finals. That sent Oklahoma City to the NBA Finals for the first time.

Despite his success, James was traded to the Houston Rockets after the 2011–2012 season. The trade gave James a new start. He became a key player for the Rockets.

James tries to block a shot during a 2011 game.

HARDEN DOES IT ALL

Harden takes a shot over the Golden State Warriors' Klay Thompson during a 2018 game.

When Harden is on the basketball court, opponents know to keep a close eye on him. He is one of the best scorers in the NBA. He is a gifted shooter but can **drive** to the hoop as well. This makes him very hard to stop.

Harden tries to get around Ricky Rubio of the Utah Jazz.

Harden is one of the best three-point shooters in the NBA. He made the most three-point shots in the league during the 2017–2018 season. He also led the league in three-pointers attempted.

Harden's teammates expect him to take a lot of shots. Half of the shots Harden takes are three-pointers. When he takes two-point shots, he prefers to drive to the hoop. He does not usually take two-point **jump shots**. To get to the rim, Harden often uses a move called the Euro step.

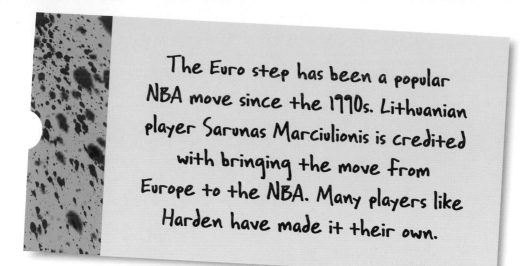

The Euro step has been a popular NBA move since the 1990s. Lithuanian player Sarunas Marciulionis is credited with bringing the move from Europe to the NBA. Many players like Harden have made it their own.

The Euro step is used to beat defenders. With a defender running at him, Harden fakes a step toward the defender. That gets the opponent going in one direction. Harden then takes a powerful step in the opposite direction. Harden has perfected this move to get wide-open shots.

Harden stands at six foot five (2 m) and 218 pounds (99 kg). But he was not always so big and strong. In college, Harden did not take nutrition seriously. He ate whatever he wanted.

Harden smiles during practice.

When he got to the
NBA, he could no
longer eat that way.
The Thunder training
staff taught Harden
the importance of
eating right. Harden
noticed a change
in his game. Now
he eats only **lean**
proteins such as
chicken and fish.

Harden takes a break
to rest during a game.

Harden says he still likes desserts. But he tries to limit
the amount of sweets he eats.

Harden spent a lot of time at the gym before his MVP
season. One thing he worked on with his strength coach
was **conditioning**. Harden plays a lot. He wanted to
make sure he would be healthy for the long season.

On a normal gym day, Harden works with his strength
coach for an hour. Then he hits the court and trains
with his basketball skills coach for an hour. After that,
he usually plays in a **pickup game** for about two hours.
Even in the **off-season**, Harden never stops working to
get better.

HARDEN OFF
THE COURT

Harden high-fives a fan on his way back to the locker room after a game.

It's no wonder that Harden is a Rockets' fan favorite. He is one of the most exciting players in the NBA. And he has helped the Rockets become one of the best teams in the Western Conference.

Harden participated in a charity dinner in 2018 to help raise money for people in need living in Houston.

But Harden also gives to the Houston community. When Hurricane Harvey hit the area in 2017, Harden gave one million dollars. The **donation** helped some families whose homes were damaged in the storm. He also helped serve Thanksgiving meals to families who were affected.

Harden organizes events around the holidays for people in need. He has paid for shopping sprees for families to purchase Christmas gifts.

The 3TheHardenWay Foundation is Harden's personal charity organization. It works to help Houston students succeed. This includes providing **scholarships** to help students pay for college.

"I think about this more than anything," Harden said about charity work. "I think about basketball, too, of course, but I think about how I can give back and what I can do all the time."

Outside of basketball and charity work, Harden enjoys being himself. He loves fashion and often wears fun outfits. He wore a cow-patterned suit to accept his 2018 MVP award. Harden sometimes posts his fashion choices on Instagram for his fans to see.

Harden is known for his fun sense of style.

The Start of the Beard

Harden's bushy beard is something that fans know and love. He first grew the beard because he got tired of shaving. But then he started to like how it looked.

Harden's beard became famous when he played for the Thunder. The team sold T-shirts with the words "Fear the Beard." A fan even started a Twitter account just for the beard. Harden has said he will never shave it off.

Harden shows off his famous beard.

FEAR THE BEARD

Harden takes a shot in a game against the Los Angeles Lakers.

The Thunder thought they got a good deal in trading Harden. They received two first-round draft picks, plus some other players. But none of them came close to replacing Harden.

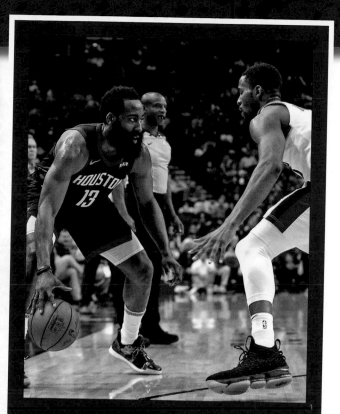
Harden dribbles the ball against Maurice Harkless of the Portland Trail Blazers.

Harden started very few games in Oklahoma City. He has started almost every game in Houston. With more playing time, Harden set several career records, and he made his first All-Star team. Harden finally had a chance to show his skills.

"It's all happened so fast, but I'm just humble about it and trying to stay on path and just focus on what I can do and what's got me here," Harden said during his first year in Houston. In February 2013 Harden scored a career-high 46 points in a 122–119 win against the Thunder.

Harden laughs on the sidelines as the Rockets warm up before a game against the Los Angeles Lakers.

In 2014–2015 and 2015–2016, Harden played so much that he led the league in minutes played. He only missed three games from 2014 through 2017. And that doesn't even include the playoffs. With Harden, the Rockets were making the playoffs every year.

Harden talks to a referee during a game.

The 2017–2018 season was special for Harden and the Rockets. Harden's MVP effort led the Rockets to their best season since winning the NBA title in 1995. They won 65 games and made it all the way to the Western Conference finals, where they faced the Golden State Warriors.

Some of Harden's fans wear fake beards
or hold signs to support him.

Harden struggled with his shooting during the playoffs. He and the Rockets suffered a 126–85 defeat in Game 3. The Warriors took a 2–1 lead. But Harden bounced back with 30 points in Game 4, which the Rockets won. Then Houston won Game 5. They were just one win away from getting back to the NBA Finals.

Unfortunately for the Rockets, the Warriors went on to win Games 6 and 7. But Harden scored the most points for the Rockets in both games. There was no denying Harden was a superstar. Some people say he's the best player in the NBA. But winning a championship would make him a legend. Harden plans to keep working until he meets that goal.

Harden takes a shot during a game against the Golden State Warriors in 2018.

All-Star Stats

Harden has climbed his way up to be one of the Rockets' all-time leaders. During the 2018–2019 season, Harden moved up to third place in points scored with the Houston Rockets:

Houston Rockets Top Scorers

1. Hakeem Olajuwon: 26,511
2. Calvin Murphy: 17,949
3. James Harden: 13,625
4. Rudy Tomjanovich: 13,383
5. Elvin Hayes: 11,762
6. Moses Malone: 11,119
7. Yao Ming: 9,247
8. Robert Reid: 8,823
9. Mike Newlin: 8,480
10. Otis Thorpe: 8,177

Source Notes

6. Ohm Youngmisuk, "Rockets' James Harden Awarded NBA's MVP After Career Season," *ESPN.com*, June 26, 2018, http://www.espn.com/nba/story/_/id/23908102/james-harden-houston-rockets-garners-mvp-award-career-season.

10. Marc J. Spears, "Rockets' James Harden and His Mom on How Sports Shaped the MVP Candidate," *The Undefeated*, May 5, 2017, https://theundefeated.com/features/rockets-james-harden-and-mom-sports-shaped-mvp-candidate/.

20. Jenny Dial Creech, "James Harden's Excited to Give Back to the City in His Way," *Houston Chronicle*, August 18, 2018, https://www.houstonchronicle.com/sports/columnists/dialcreech/article/James-Harden-s-excited-to-give-back-to-the-city-13166209.php.

23. Sean Amick, "James Harden Embraces Rise to Superstar with Rockets," *USA Today*, February 14, 2013, https://www.usatoday.com/story/sports/nba/2013/02/14/james-harden-houston-rockets-nba-all-star/1921159/.

Glossary

breakout: related to a performance that makes others take notice

bushy: thick and full

charity: related to an organization that raises money for a certain cause

conditioning: the process of becoming stronger and healthier with regular exercise and diet

donation: a gift, usually of money, to an organization such as a charity

drive: in basketball, to make a strong and determined run to the basket

jump shots: shots taken from the floor in which a player jumps and releases the ball

lean: meat with little fat

off-season: time outside of a regular sports season

pickup game: a casual game of basketball that is not part of any official competition

prospect: an athlete expected to be a good player in the future

scholarships: money given to students to pay for their college tuition

upset: to win a game unexpectedly

Further Information

Fishman, Jon M. *James Harden*. Minneapolis: Lerner
    Publications, 2016.

James Harden Official Site
http://jamesharden.com

James Harden Rockets Bio
http://www.nba.com/players/james/harden/201935

James Harden Stats
https://www.basketball-reference.com/players/h/hardeja01.
html

Mattern, Joanne. *James Harden*. Hallandale, FL: Mitchell
    Lane Publishers, 2018.

Scheff, Matt. *James Harden*: *Basketball Star*. Lake Elmo, MN:
    Focus Readers, 2018.

Index

Photo Acknowledgments

The images in this book are used with the permission of: © Tim Warner/Getty Images Sport/Getty Images, pp. 4–5, 8, 15, 17, 18, 23; © Kevin Winter/Turner Sports/Getty Images Entertainment/Getty Images, p. 6; © Phillip Faraone/adidas/Getty Images Entertainment/Getty Images, p. 7; © Seth Poppel/Yearbook Library, p. 9; © Joe Robbins/Getty Images Sport/Getty Images, p. 11; © Mark J. Terrill/AFP/Getty Images, p. 12; © AAron Ontiveroz/The Denver Post/Getty Images, p. 13; © Nhat V. Meyer/Bay Area News Group/MediaNews Group/The Mercury News/Digital First Media/Getty Images, p. 14; © Jayne Kamin-Oncea/Getty Images Sport/Getty Images, p. 16; © Bob Levey/Getty Images Entertainment/Getty Images, pp. 19, 24; © Pascal Le Segretain/Getty Images Entertainment/Getty Images, p. 20; © Tom Szczerbowski/New Era Cap Co./Getty Images Entertainment/Getty Images, p. 21; © Harry How/Getty Images Sport/Getty Images, p. 22; © Michael Reaves/Getty Images Sport/Getty Images, p. 25; © Ronald Martinez/Getty Images Sport/Getty Images, pp. 26, 27.

Front cover: © Ronald Martinez/Getty Images Sport/Getty Images.